my first fruits
in arabic

translated by Nada Elshabrawy

polyglot kids

تفاح

tuffāḥ

apple

كمثرى

kummathrā

pear

عنب

inab

grape

تين

tīn

fig

توت

tūt

mulberry

برقوق

burqūq

plum

كَرَز

karaz

cherry

خوخ

khawkh

peach

رمّان

rummān

pomegranate

شمّام

šammām

melon

© 2025 by Polyglot Kids Books / World Poetry Books
Photography © 2025 by Sebastian Fröhlich

Series editors: Peter Constantine & Hannes Schumacher
Translated into Arabic by Nada Elshabrawy
Photography: Sebastian Fröhlich
Design: Hannes Schumacher & Sebastian Fröhlich
ISBN: 978-1-967821-01-3

Polyglot Kids Books is an imprint of World Poetry Books, Inc. New York.

www.ingramcontent.com/pod-product-compliance
Lightning Source LLC
Chambersburg PA
CBHW062022050526
44107CB00106B/942